STRUM & SING
UKULELE

THE Beatles

Cover photo: Getty Images / Mark and Colleen Hayward / Contributor

ISBN 978-1-4950-9442-2

HAL•LEONARD®
CORPORATION
7777 W. BLUEMOUND RD. P.O. BOX 13819 MILWAUKEE, WI 53213

Visit Hal Leonard Online at
www.halleonard.com

All My Loving

Words and Music by
John Lennon and Paul McCartney

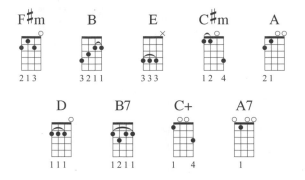

Verse 1

‖F#m |B
Close your eyes and I'll kiss you,

|E |C#m
To - morrow I'll miss you,

|A |F#m |D |B7
Re - member, I'll always be true.

|F#m |B
And then while I'm a - way

|E |C#m
I'll write home every day,

|A |B |E |
And I'll send all my loving to you.

N.C.   ‖F#m |B

Verse 2

I'll pre - tend that I'm kissing

|E |C#m
The lips I am missing

|A |F#m |D |B7
And hope that my dreams will come true.

|F#m |B
And then while I'm a - way

|E |C#m
I'll write home every day,

|A |B |E |
And I'll send all my loving to you.

Chorus 1

N.C.   ‖ C#m |C+ |E |
   All my loving,   I will send to you,
     |C#m |C+ |E | N.C. ‖
All my loving, darling, I'll be true.

Solo

|A7 |E | |
|B7 |E |

Verse 3

N.C.   ‖F#m |B
Close your eyes and I'll kiss you,
   |E |C#m
To - morrow I'll miss you,
   |A |F#m |D |B7
Re - member, I'll always be true.
    |F#m |B
And then while I'm a - way
    |E |C#m
I'll write home every day,
    |A |B |E |
And I'll send all my loving to you.

Chorus 2

N.C.   ‖C#m |C+ |E |
   All my loving,   I will send to you,
   |C#m |C+ |E |
All my loving, darling, I'll be true.
   |C#m |
All my loving,
   |E |
All my loving, oo-ooh,
   |C#m |
All my loving
      |E | ‖
I will send to you.

All You Need Is Love

Words and Music by
John Lennon and Paul McCartney

G   D   C   D7   Em

D7*   Bm7   A7   B7   Em7

Intro

|G   D |G |C   D7 |

G   D |Em |
Love, love,   love,

G   D |Em |
Love, love,   love,

D7   G |D7* |
Love, love,   love.

D   D7* |Bm7   D   ‖

Verse 1

G   D |Em |
　　There's nothing you can do that can't be done,

G   D |Em7 |
　　Nothing you can sing that can't be sung,

D7   G
　　Nothing you can say,

**　　　　　　　　　　　　　|D   D7* |**
But you can learn how to play the game,

**　|D   D7* |Bm7   D   ‖**
　It's easy.

Verse 2

```
G           D              |Em        |
  Nothing you can make that can't be made,
G        D          |Em           |
  No one you can save that can't be saved,
D7              G
  Nothing you can do,
              |D                    D7
But you can learn how to be you in time,
  |D   D7*  |Bm7  D          ||
It's easy.
```

Chorus 1

```
G       A7   |D    D7      |
  All you need is love,
G       A7   |D    D7      |
  All you need is love,
G       B7   |Em  Em7      |
  All you need is love, love,
C       D7              |G        ||
  Love is all you need.
```

Solo

```
 G    D   |Em         |
(Love, love,   love.)
 G    D   |Em         |
(Love, love,   love.)
 D7   G    |D   D7*  |
(Love, love,   love.)
 D    D7*  |Bm7  D        ||
```

Chorus 2   *Repeat Chorus 1*

Verse 3

```
G              D              |Em        |
  There's nothing you can know that isn't known,
G                  D          |Em        |
  There's nothing you can see that isn't shown,
D7                  G
  There's nowhere you can be
      |D                    D7
That isn't where you're meant to be,
      |D    D7*  |Bm7  D        ||
It's easy.
```

Chorus 3   *Repeat Chorus 1*

Chorus 4   *Repeat Chorus 1*

Outro

```
G          |
  Love is all  you need. (Love is all you need.)
          |                              |
Love is all  you need. (Love is all you need.)
||:        |
  Love is all  you need. (Love is all you need.)
          |                        :|| Repeat and fade
Love is all  you need. (Love is all you need.)
```

Eight Days a Week

Words and Music by
John Lennon and Paul McCartney

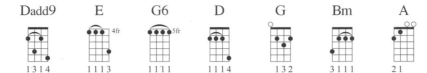

Intro   **Dadd9** |**E** |**G6** |**Dadd9**   ‖

Verse 1
     D |**E** |
Ooh, I need your love, babe;
G |**D** |
Guess you know it's true.
              |**E** |
Hope you need my love, babe,
G |**D**   ‖
Just like I need you.

Chorus 1
Bm |**G** |
Hold me, love me,
Bm |**E**
Hold me, love me.
 |**D** |**E** |
I ain't got nothing but love, babe,
G |**D**   ‖
   Eight days a week.

Verse 2

```
D            |E              |
Love  you  every  day,  girl,
G                    |D           |
Always  on  my  mind.
                     |E           |
One  thing  I  can  say,  girl,
G                    |D           ||
Love  you  all  the  time.
```

Chorus 2   *Repeat Chorus 1*

Bridge 1

```
A             |
Eight  days  a  week,
 |Bm      |        |
I  love      you.
E             |
Eight  days  a  week
 |G            |A              ||
Is  not  enough  to  show  I  care.
```

Verse 3   *Repeat Verse 1*

Chorus 3   *Repeat Chorus 1*

Bridge 2	*Repeat Bridge 1*
Verse 4	*Repeat Verse 2*

Chorus 4

Bm   **|G** |
Hold me, love me,
Bm   **|E**
Hold me, love me.
 |D   **|E** |
I ain't got nothing but love, babe,
G   **|D** |
  Eight days a week.
G   **|D** |
  Eight days a week.
G   **|D** ||
  Eight days a week.

Outro   **Dadd9** **|E**   **|G6**   **|Dadd9** ||

And I Love Her

Words and Music by
John Lennon and Paul McCartney

F#m   E6   C#m   A   B   E   G#m   B7
3 4 2 1   1 1 1 1   3 1 1 1   1 2 4 3   1 2 4 3   1 1 1 4   1 3 4 2   1 2 1 1

Gm   Dm   Bb   C   F   F6   D
2 3 1   2 3 1   3 2 1 1   4   2 1   2 3 1   1 1 1

Intro

| F#m | | E6 | ‖

Verse 1

| F#m | C#m |
I give her all my love,
| F#m | C#m |
That's all I do,
| F#m | C#m |
And if you saw my love,
A | B
You'd love her too,
| E | ‖
I love her.

Verse 2

| F#m | C#m |
She gives me everything,
| F#m | C#m |
And tenderly,
| F#m | C#m |
The kiss my lover brings,
A | B
She brings to me,
| E | ‖
And I love her.

Bridge

C♯m |B |
A love like ours
C♯m |G♯m |
Could never die
C♯m |G♯m |
As long as I
         |B |B7 ||
Have you near me.

Verse 3

F♯m |C♯m |
Bright are the stars that shine,
F♯m |C♯m |
Dark is the sky,
F♯m |C♯m |
I know this love of mine
A |B
Will never die,
      |E | ||
And I love her.

Guitar Solo

|Gm |Dm |Gm |Dm |Gm |
|Dm |B♭ |C |F | ||

Verse 4

Gm |Dm |
Bright are the stars that shine,
Gm |Dm |
Dark is the sky,
Gm |Dm |
I know this love of mine
B♭ |C
Will never die,
      |F | ||
And I love her.

Outro

|Gm | |F6 | |
|Gm | |D ||

Blackbird

Words and Music by
John Lennon and Paul McCartney

Intro

G   Am7   G* |G** | ‖

Verse 1

G   Am7   G* |G** | |
Blackbird singing in the dead of night,
C   C♯° |D   D♯° |Em |Em(maj7) |
Take these broken wings __ and learn __ to fly.
D   C♯° |C |Cm |
All your life,
G |A7 |D7sus4 |G   ‖
You were only wait - ing for this mo - ment to arise.

Interlude 1

|C   G |A7 |D7sus4 |G   ‖

Verse 2

G   Am7   G* |G** | |
Blackbird singing in the dead of night,
C   C♯° |D   D♯° |Em |Em(maj7) |
Take these sunken eyes __ and learn __ to see.
D   C♯° |C |Cm |
All your life,
G |A7 |D7sus4 |G   ‖
You were only wait - ing for this mo - ment to be free.

Bridge 1

F   C |Dm C |B♭6 |C |
Black - bird, _____ fly.

F   C |Dm C |B♭6 |A7
Black - bird, _____ fly.

          |D7sus4   ‖
Into the light _____ of a dark black

Interlude 2

G   Am7 G* |G** |C C#° D D#° |Em   Em(maj7) |
night.

D   C#° |C   Cm |G   A7 |D7sus4   G   ‖

Bridge 2

Repeat Bridge 1

Interlude 3

G   Am7 G* |G* | | |
night.

D   Am7 G* C |G*   A7 D7sus4   ‖

Verse 3

G   Am7   G* |G** | |
Blackbird singing in the dead of night,

C   C#° |D   D#° |Em |Em(maj7) |
Take these broken wings __ and learn __ to fly.

D C#° |C |Cm |
All your life,

G |A7 |D7sus4 |G |
You were only wait - ing for this mo - ment to arise.

C   G |A7 |D7sus4 |G |
You were on - ly wait - ing for this mo - ment to arise.

C   G |A7 |D7sus4 |G   ‖
You were on - ly waiting __ for this mo - ment to arise.

Can't Buy Me Love

Words and Music by
John Lennon and Paul McCartney

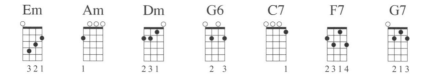

Intro

‖**Em** |**Am** |**Em** |**Am**
Can't buy me love, _____ love,

|**Dm** |**G6**
Can't buy me love.

Verse 1

‖**C7** |
I'll buy you a diamond ring, my friend,

| |
If it makes you feel al - right.

|**F7** |
I'll get you anything, my friend,

|**C7** |
If it makes you feel al - right.

|**G7** |**F7** |
'Cause I don't care too   much for money, 'cause

|**C7**
Money can't buy me love.

Verse 2

‖**C7** |
I'll give you all I've got to give,

| |
If you say you love me too.

|**F7** |
I may not have a lot to give,

|**C7** |
But what I've got I'll give to you.

|**G7** |**F7** |
I   don't care too   much for money, 'cause

|**C7**
Money can't buy me love.

Chorus 1

```
                    ‖Em  |Am
Can't buy me love,
       |C7            |
Ev - 'rybody tells me so.
                 |Em  |Am   |
Can't buy me love,
Dm        |G6          ‖
No, no, no, no.
```

Verse 3

```
         C7                 |
Say you don't need no diamond rings
         |          |
And I'll be satis - fied.
      |F7              |
Tell me that you want the kind of things
      |C7           |
That money just can't buy.
 |G7            |F7  N.C.        |
I   don't care too   much for money,
F7                     |C7     |        ‖
Money can't buy me love.
```

Solo

```
C7          |           |           |           |
F7          |           |C7         |           |
G7          |F7         |C7         |
```

Chorus 2

Repeat Chorus 1

Verse 4

```
         C7                 |
Say you don't need no diamond rings
         |          |
And I'll be satis - fied.
      |F7              |
Tell me that you want the kind of things
      |C7           |
That money just can't buy.
 |G7            |F7  N.C.        |
I   don't care too   much for money,
F7                     |C7     |
Money can't buy me love.
```

Outro

```
                 ‖Em  |Am  |Em  |Am
Can't buy me love, _____ love,
             ‖Dm        |G6     |
Can't buy me love.
C7      |        ‖
Oh.
```

Come Together

Words and Music by
John Lennon and Paul McCartney

Dm7   A   G7   Bm   Bm7   G

Intro

‖:**Dm7** | :‖
(Shoot me.   Shoot me.)

Verse 1

Dm7 |
Here come old flat top, he come grooving up slowly,

| |
He got joo joo eyeball, he one holy roller,

|**A** | |
He got hair down to his knees,

G7 N.C. | ‖
Got to be a joker, he just do what he please.

Interlude 1

‖:**Dm7** | :‖
(Shoot me.   Shoot me.)

Verse 2

Dm7 |
He wear no shoe shine, he got toe jam football,

| |
He got monkey finger, he shoot Coca Cola,

|**A** | | |
He say, "I know you, you know me."

G7 N.C. |
One thing I can tell you is you got to be free.

Chorus 1

‖**Bm**
Come togeth - er,

Bm7 |**G**   **A**
Right   now,

N.C. |
Over me.

Dm7 | | | ‖

Verse 3

Dm7 |
  He bag production, he got walrus gumboot,
      | |
He got Ono sideboard, he one spinal cracker,
      |A | |
He got   feet down below his knee,
G7   N.C. |
Hold you in his armchair, you can feel his disease.

Chorus 2

                    ‖Bm
Come togeth - er,
Bm7 |G   A
Right   now,
N.C. |Dm7 | ‖
Over me.   Right!

Solo

Dm7 | | | |
                            Come.
A | | |Dm7 | ‖

Verse 4

Dm7 |
  He roller coaster, he got early warning,
      | |
He got muddy water, he one mojo filter,
        |A | |
He say,   "One and one and one is three."
G7   N.C. |
Got to be good looking 'cause he's so hard to see.

Chorus 3

                    ‖Bm
Come togeth - er,
Bm7 |G   A
Right   now,
N.C. ‖
Over

Outro

Dm7 | | | | |
me.   Oh!
‖: | :‖ *Repeat and fade*
  Come together, yeah!

Day Tripper

Words and Music by
John Lennon and Paul McCartney

E7   A7   F#7   A7*   G#7   C#7   B7

1 2 3   1   2 3 1 4   2 3 1 4   2 3 1 4   1 2 1 1   1 2 1 1

Intro   **E7** | ‖: | | | :‖

Verse 1

E7 |
Got a good reason

| | |
For taking the easy way out.
A7 |
Got a good reason
|**E7** |
For taking the easy way out, now.

Chorus 1

‖ **F#7** | |
She was a day   tripper,

|
One way ticket, yeah.
|**A7*** |**G#7** |**C#7**
It took me so   long to find out,
|**B7** ‖
And I found out.

Interlude 1   **E7** | | | ‖

Verse 2

E7 | |
She's a big teaser,

| | |
She took me half the way there.
A7 | |
She's a big teaser,
E7 |
She took me half the way there, now.

Chorus 2   *Repeat Chorus 1*

Solo   ‖: **B7** | | | :‖ *Play 3 times*

Interlude 2   *Repeat Interlude 1*

Verse 3

E7 | |
Tried to please her,

| |
She only played one night stands.
A7 | |
Tried to please her,
E7 |
She only played one night stands, now.

Chorus 3

|**F♯7** | |
She was a day   tripper,

|
Sunday driver, yeah.
|**A7*** |**G♯7** |**C♯7**
It took me so   long to find out,
|**B7** ‖
And I found out.

Outro

‖: **E7** | | | :‖

‖: | | | |
   Day tripper,   day tripper, yeah.
| | | :‖ *Repeat and fade*
Day tripper,   day tripper, yeah.

Eleanor Rigby

Words and Music by
John Lennon and Paul McCartney

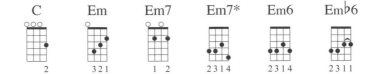

Intro

C | |**Em** | |
Ah, look at all the lonely peo - ple!
C | |**Em** | ||
Ah, look at all the lonely peo - ple!

Verse 1

Em |
Eleanor Rigby,

| |**C** |
Picks up the rice in the church where a wedding has been,
Em |
Lives in a dream.

|
Waits at the window,

| **Em7** |**C** |
Wearing a face that she keeps in a jar by the door,
Em ||
Who is it for?

Chorus 1

Em7* |**Em6** |**Em♭6** |**Em** |
All the lonely people, where do they all come from?
Em7* |**Em6** |**Em♭6** |**Em** ||
All the lonely people, where do they all be - long?

Verse 2

Em |

Father McKenzie,

| |C

Writing the words of a ser - mon that no one will hear,

| Em |

No one comes near.

|

Look at him working,

| Em7 |C |

Darning his socks in the night when there's nobody there,

Em ‖

What does he care?

Chorus 2　　　　　　　　　*Repeat Chorus 1*

Bridge

C | |Em |

Ah, look at all the lonely peo - ple!

C | |Em ‖

Ah, look at all the lonely peo - ple!

Verse 3

Em |

Eleanor Rigby,

| |C |

Died in the church and was bur - ied along with her name,

Em |

Nobody came.

|

Father McKenzie,

| Em7 |C |

Wiping the dirt from his hands as he walks from the grave,

Em ‖

No one was saved.

Chorus 3　　　　　　　　　*Repeat Chorus 1*

The Fool on the Hill

Words and Music by
John Lennon and Paul McCartney

D6	Em/D	Em7	A7	Bm7	Dm	B♭	C7	Dm7
1 1 1 1	1 2	2 3 1 4	1 3 2 4	3 1 1 4	2 3 1	3 2 1 1	1	2 3 1 4

Intro |D6 ‖

Verse 1

D6 |Em/D
Day after day, a - lone on a hill,

   |D6 |Em/D
The man with the foolish grin is keeping perfectly still.

Pre-Chorus 1

  ‖Em7   A7
But nobody wants to know him,

    |D6   Bm7
They can see that he's just a fool.

   |Em7   A7
And he never gives an an - swer;

Chorus 1

   ‖Dm   B♭   Dm
But the fool   on the hill

    |B♭
Sees the sun going down,

   |C7
And the eyes in his head

    |Dm   Dm7 |D6   ‖
See the world spinning 'round.

Verse 2

     D6   **|Em/D**
Well on the way; head in a cloud,

   |D6   **|Em/D**
The man of a thousand voices talking perfectly loud.

Pre-Chorus 2

     ‖Em7   **A7**
But nobody ever hears him,

         |D6   **Bm7**
Or the sound he appears to make.

    |Em7   **A7**   **‖**
And he never seems to notice;

Chorus 2   *Repeat Chorus 1*

Solo   **D6**   **|Em/D**   **|D6**   **|Em/D**

Pre-Chorus 3

     ‖Em7   **A7**
And nobody seems to like him,

         |D6   **Bm7**
They can tell what he wants to do.

    |Em7   **A7**
And he never shows his feelings;

Chorus 3

     ‖Dm   **B♭**   **Dm**
But the fool   on the hill

       |B♭
Sees the sun going down,

      |C7
And the eyes in his head

      |Dm   **Dm7** **|D6**   **‖**
See the world spinning 'round.   Oh.

Interlude

D6 |Em/D |
(Oh,   oh.

D6 |Em/D
'Round, 'round, 'round, 'round, 'round.)

Pre-Chorus 4

‖Em7   A7
And he never listens to them,

|D6   Bm7 |
He knows that they're the fool.

Em7   A7
They don't like him;

Chorus 4

‖Dm Bb   Dm
The fool   on the hill

        |Bb
Sees the sun going down,

     |C7
And the eyes in his head

       |Dm   Dm7 | D6   ‖
See the world spinning 'round.

Outro

‖: D6 |
   (Oh,

Em/D
'Round, 'round, 'round,

         :‖ *Repeat and fade*
'Round, and…)

Golden Slumbers

Words and Music by
John Lennon and Paul McCartney

Am7   Dm   G7   C   E7   Am   Asus2   F

Intro

Am7 ‖

Verse 1

Am7 |Dm | |
Once there was a way to get back home - ward,
G7 |C
Once there was a way to get back home.
E7 |Am Asus2| Dm |
Sleep, pretty dar - ling, do not cry,
G7 |C   ‖
    And I will sing a lulla - by.

Chorus

C |F |C |
Golden slum - bers fill your eyes,
          |F |C
Smiles a - wake you when you rise.
E7 |Am Asus2 |Dm |
Sleep, pretty dar - ling, do not cry,
G7 |C   ‖
    And I will sing a lulla - by.

Verse 2

Am7 |Dm | |
Once there was a way to get back home - ward,
G7 |C
Once there was a way to get back home.
E7 |Am Asus2 |Dm |
Sleep, pretty dar - ling, do not cry,
G7 |C   ‖
    And I will sing a lulla - by.

Good Day Sunshine

Words and Music by
John Lennon and Paul McCartney

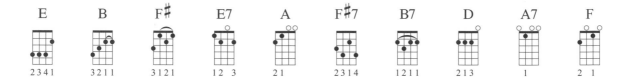

Intro

E | | | ‖

Chorus 1

B   F# | |B   F# | |
Good day sun - shine. Good day sun - shine.
E   E7 |
Good day sun - shine.

Verse 1

N.C.   ‖A   F#7 |B7 |
    I need to laugh,   and when the sun is out,
E7 |A
I've got something I can   laugh about.
    | F#7 |B7 |
I feel good   in a special way,
E7 |A   ‖
I'm in love and it's a   sunny day.

Chorus 2

Repeat Chorus 1

Verse 2

N.C.   ‖A F#7 |B7 |
   We take a walk,   the sun is shining down,
E7 |A   ‖
Burns my feet as they touch the ground.

Solo

D   B7 |E7 |A7 |D   ‖

Chorus 3

Repeat Chorus 1

Verse 3

N.C.   ‖A F#7 |B7 |
   Then we lie   beneath a shady tree,
E7 |A
I love her and she's loving me.
        | F#7 |B7 |
She feels good,   she knows she's looking fine.
E7 |A   ‖
I'm so proud to know that   she is mine.

Chorus 4

Repeat Chorus 1

Chorus 5

B   F# | |B   F# | |
Good day sun - shine. Good day sun - shine.
E |E7 |
Good day sun - shine.
‖: F | :‖ ***Repeat and fade***
   Good day sun - shine.

Good Night

Words and Music by
John Lennon and Paul McCartney

Gmaj7   C   G   Bm7   Am7   D7

D   Gmaj7sus4   A7   Dm7   G7

Intro

Gmaj7 C |Gmaj7 C |G   C |
G   C |G   Bm7 |Am7   D7   ‖

Verse 1

G   Bm7 |Am7 |
Now it's time to say good night,

Bm7 Am7 |C   D |
Good night, sleep tight.

G   Bm7 |Am7 |
Now the sun turns out his light,

Bm7 Am7 |C   D |
Good night, sleep tight.

Gmaj7   Gmaj7sus4 |Gmaj7 Gmaj7sus4 |
Dream sweet dreams for   me,

G   C |G   C   ‖
Dream sweet dreams for you.

Verse 2

```
G         Bm7   |Am7           |
```
Close your eyes and I'll close mine,

```
Bm7  Am7 |C    D       |
```
Good night, sleep tight.

```
G         Bm7   |Am7           |
```
Now the moon be - gins to shine,

```
Bm7  Am7 |C    D       |
```
Good night, sleep tight.

```
Gmaj7       Gmaj7sus4 |Gmaj7  Gmaj7sus4 |
```
Dream sweet dreams for   me,

```
                C        |G      C        ||
```
Dream sweet dreams for you.


```
G  Am7 |A7  Dm7 |G7   C    |D     Am7  D7  ||
```
Bridge   Mm,   mm,   mm.


```
G         Bm7   |Am7           |
```
Verse 3   Close your eyes and I'll close mine,

```
Bm7  Am7 |C    D       |
```
Good night, sleep tight.

```
G         Bm7   |Am7           |
```
Now the sun turns out his light,

```
Bm7  Am7 |C    D       |
```
Good night, sleep tight.

```
Gmaj7       Gmaj7sus4 |Gmaj7  Gmaj7sus4  |
```
Dream sweet dreams for   me,

```
G         C       |G   C        ||
```
Dream sweet dreams for you.


```
G  Bm7 |Am7  D7        |
```
Outro   *Good night,*

```
G                       Bm7
```
  Good night, ev'rybody.

```
          |Am7
```
Ev'ry - body ev'rywhere,

```
          D7    |G       ||
```
Good night.
```
```

Got to Get You into My Life

Words and Music by
John Lennon and Paul McCartney

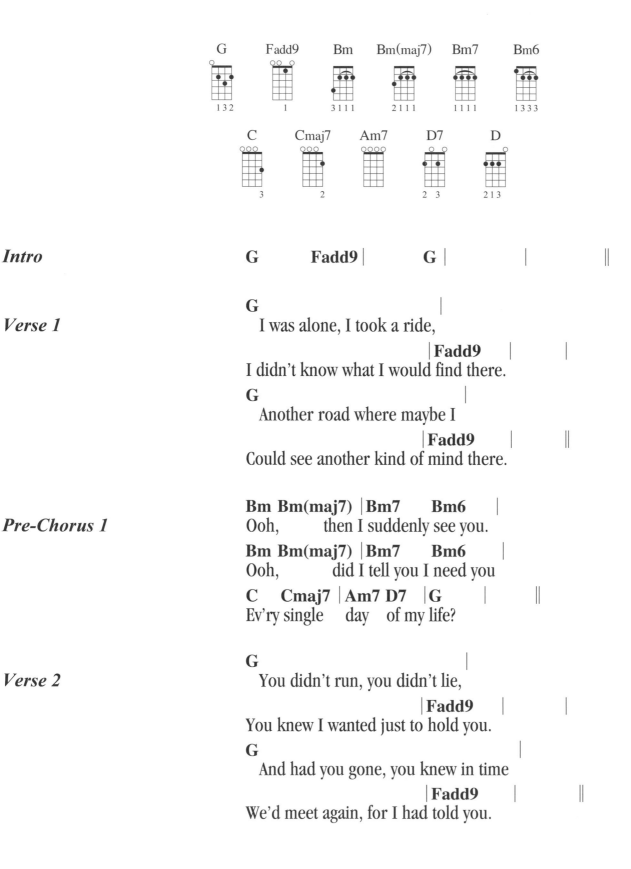

Intro   G   Fadd9 | G | | ‖

Verse 1

G |
  I was alone, I took a ride,
                                      |Fadd9 | |
I didn't know what I would find there.
G |
  Another road where maybe I
                                      |Fadd9 | ‖
Could see another kind of mind there.

Pre-Chorus 1

Bm Bm(maj7) |Bm7   Bm6 |
Ooh,   then I suddenly see you.
Bm Bm(maj7) |Bm7   Bm6 |
Ooh,   did I tell you I need you
C   Cmaj7 |Am7 D7 |G | ‖
Ev'ry single   day   of my life?

Verse 2

G |
  You didn't run, you didn't lie,
                                      |Fadd9 | |
You knew I wanted just to hold you.
G |
  And had you gone, you knew in time
                                      |Fadd9 | ‖
We'd meet again, for I had told you.

Pre-Chorus 2

Bm Bm(maj7) |Bm7   Bm6 |
Ooh,   you were meant to be near me.

Bm Bm(maj7) |Bm7   Bm6 |
Ooh,   and I want you to hear me,

C   Cmaj7 |Am7 D7 |G | ‖
Say we'll be to - gether ev'ry day.

Chorus 1

G |C | |D |G | ‖
Got to get you into my life!

Verse 3

G |
  What can I do, what can I be?

              |Fadd9 |
When I'm with you, I want to stay there.

G |
  If I am true I'll never leave,

           |Fadd9 | ‖
And if I do, I know the way there.

Pre-Chorus 3

Repeat Pre-Chorus 1

Chorus 2

G |C | |D |
Got to get you into my life!

G | | Fadd9 |C G |
   | |C | |D |G |
I've got to get you into my life!

Outro

         ‖
I was alone, I took a ride,

     | |
I didn't know what I would find there.

    |
An - other road where maybe I

     | |
Could see another kind of mind there.

     | |
Then I suddenly see you,

     | |
Did I tell you I need you

        ‖ *Fade out*
Ev'ry single day…

A Hard Day's Night

Words and Music by
John Lennon and Paul McCartney

G7sus4   G   C   F   D   Bm   Em   D7   Fadd9

Intro

G7sus4

Verse 1

‖ G   C |G
It's been a hard day's night,

   |F |G
And I've been working like a dog.

   | C |G
It's been a hard day's night,

   |F |G
I should be sleeping like a log.

Chorus 1

      ‖ C
But when I get home to you,

   |D
I find the things that you do,

     |G   C |G
Will make me feel al - right.

Verse 2

    ‖ G   C |G
You know I work all day,

   |F |G
To get you money to buy you things.

   | C |G
And it's worth it just to hear you say,

   |F |G
You're gonna give me ev'ry - thing.

Chorus 2

      ‖ C
So why on earth should I moan,

   |D
'Cause when I get you alone,

    |G   C |G
You know I feel O - kay.

Bridge 1

```
               ‖ Bm          |
When I'm home
Em                   | Bm        |
Ev'rything seems to be right.
               | G           |
When I'm home,
Em                   |
Feeling you holding me
C     | D7            ‖
Tight, tight, yeah.
```

Verse 3

Repeat Verse 1

Chorus 3

Repeat Chorus 1

Solo

```
| G    C  | G        | F       | G          |
| G    C  | G        | F       | G
```

Chorus 4

```
               ‖ C
So why on earth should I moan,
               | D
'Cause when I get you alone,
               | G   C  | G
You know I feel  O  -  kay.
```

Bridge 2

Repeat Bridge 1

Verse 5

Repeat Verse 1

Chorus 5

Repeat Chorus 1

Outro

```
C           ‖ G  C  | G
  You know I feel al  -  right,
C             | G  C  | Fadd9 F*  ‖
  You know I feel al  -  right.
‖: Fadd9   F      | Fadd9   F      :‖ Repeat and fade
```

Here Comes the Sun

Words and Music by
George Harrison

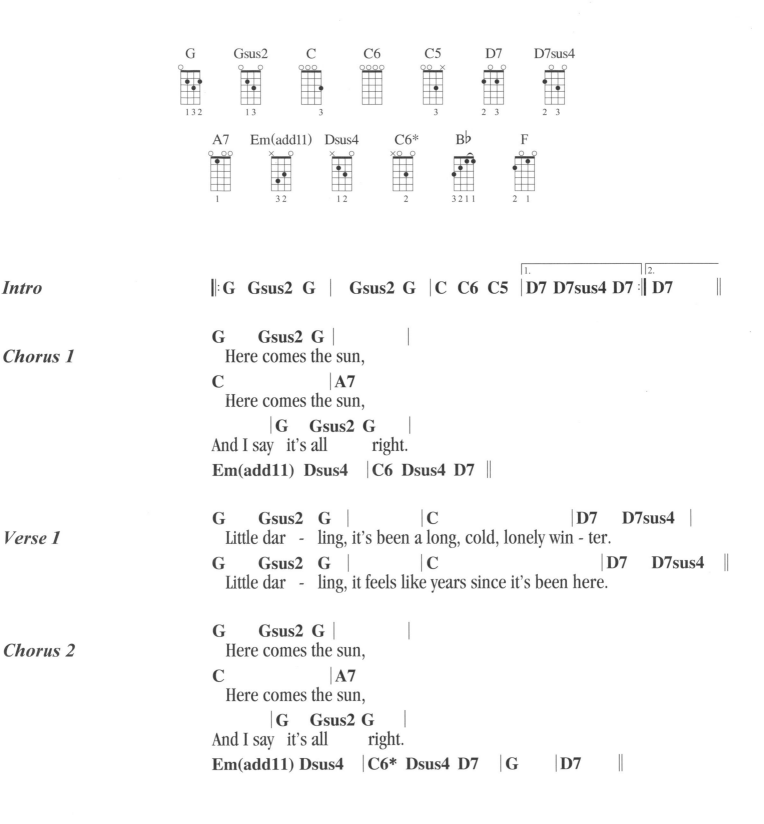

Intro

‖:G Gsus2 G | Gsus2 G |C C6 C5 |D7 D7sus4 D7 :‖ D7 ‖

Chorus 1

G   Gsus2 G | |
Here comes the sun,

C |A7
Here comes the sun,

    |G   Gsus2 G |
And I say   it's all   right.

Em(add11) Dsus4 |C6 Dsus4 D7 ‖

Verse 1

G   Gsus2 G | |C |D7   D7sus4 |
Little dar - ling, it's been a long, cold, lonely win - ter.

G   Gsus2 G | |C |D7   D7sus4 ‖
Little dar - ling, it feels like years since it's been here.

Chorus 2

G   Gsus2 G | |
Here comes the sun,

C |A7
Here comes the sun,

    |G   Gsus2 G |
And I say   it's all   right.

Em(add11) Dsus4 |C6* Dsus4 D7 |G |D7   ‖

Verse 2

```
G     Gsus2  G  |              |C                      |D7    D7sus4 |
Little dar  -  ling, the smile's re - turning to their faces,
G     Gsus2  G  |              |C                      |D7    D7sus4 ||
Little dar  -  ling, it seems like years since it's been here.
```

Chorus 3   *Repeat Chorus 2*

Bridge

```
B♭    |F    |C    |        |G     |D7     ||
‖:B♭  |F    |C    |        |G     |D7    :‖   Play 5 times
 Sun,   sun,    sun,    here it comes.
 D7    |D7sus4 |D7    |D7sus4  D7    ||
```

Verse 3

```
G     Gsus2  G  |              |C                      |D7    D7sus4 |
Little dar  -  ling, I feel that ice is slowly melt - ing.
G     Gsus2  G  |              |C                      |D7    D7sus4 ||
Little dar  -  ling, it seems like years since it's been clear.
```

Chorus 4   *Repeat Chorus 1*

Chorus 5

```
G     Gsus2  G  |          |
  Here comes the sun,
C                    |A7      |
  Here comes the sun,
G                |
  It's alright.
Em(add11)  Dsus4   |C6*  Dsus4  D7   |
G                |
  It's all right.
Em(add11)  Dsus4   |C6*  Dsus4  D7   |
B♭    F   |C       |G         ||
```

Here, There and Everywhere

Words and Music by
John Lennon and Paul McCartney

G   Bm   Bb   Am7   D7   Am   C

F#m7   B7   Em   F7   Gm   Cm

Intro

   G   **Bm** |
To lead a better life,

Bb | **Am7 D7** ‖
I need my love to be here.

Verse 1

G   **Am** |
Here,

Bm   **C** |**G Am** |
Making each day __ of the year.

Bm   **C** |**F#m7**   **B7** |
Changing my life __ with a wave __ of her hand.

F#m7   **B7** |**Em**   **Am** |**Am7 D7** ‖
Nobody can __ deny __ that there's some - thing there.

Verse 2

G   **Am** |
There,

Bm   **C** |**G Am** |
Running my hands __ through her hair.

Bm   **C** |**F#m7**   **B7** |
Both of us think - ing how good __ it can be.

F#m7   **B7** |**Em**   **Am** |**Am7 D7**
Someone is speak - ing, but she doesn't know __ he's there.

Bridge 1

```
             F7      ‖Bb          Gm
I want her ev'rywhere,
        |Cm           D7          |Gm           |
And if she's beside me, I know I need never care.
Cm          D7                    ‖
But to love her is to need her
```

Verse 3

```
             G          Am   |
Ev'rywhere.
Bm            C            |G    Am   |
Knowing that love ___ is to share.
Bm            C            |F#m7       B7      |
Each one believ - ing that love ___ never dies,
F#m7              B7    |Em          Am          |Am7  D7
Watching their eyes ___ and hoping I'm al - ways there.
```

Bridge 2

```
             F7      ‖Bb          Gm
I want her ev'rywhere,
        |Cm           D7          |Gm           |
And if she's beside me, I know I need never care.
Cm          D7                    ‖
But to love her is to need her
```

Verse 4

```
             G          Am   |
Ev'rywhere.
Bm            C            |G    Am   |
Knowing that love ___ is to share.
Bm            C            |F#m7       B7      |
Each one believ - ing that love ___ never dies.
F#m7              B7    |Em          Am          |Am7  D7
Watching her eyes ___ and hoping I'm al - ways there.
```

Outro

```
             ‖G    Am
I will be there
      |Bm       C   |
And ev'rywhere.
G     Am    |Bm        C |G         ‖
Here, there and ev'rywhere.
```

Hey Jude

Words and Music by
John Lennon and Paul McCartney

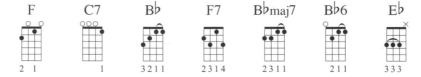

Verse 1

‖**F** |**C7**
Hey Jude, don't make it bad.

        | |**F**
Take a sad song and make it better.

        |**Bb** |**F**
Re - member to let her into your heart,

                   |**C7** |**F**
Then you can start to make it bet - ter.

Verse 2

‖**F** |**C7**
Hey Jude, don't be a - fraid.

        | |**F**
You were made to go out and get her.

        |**Bb** |**F**
The minute you let her under your skin,

                   |**C7** |**F** |
Then you be - gin to make it bet - ter.

Bridge 1

F7   ‖ B♭
 And anytime you feel the pain,

 B♭maj7 | B♭6
Hey Jude, re - frain.

    | B♭ | C7 | F |
Don't car - ry the world upon your shoul - ders.

F7 | B♭
 For well you know that it's a fool

  B♭maj7 | B♭6
Who plays it cool

    B♭ | C7 | F
By mak - ing his world a little cold - er.

    | F7 C7 | |
Na, na, na, na, na, na, na, na, na.

  ‖ F | C7

Verse 3

Hey Jude, don't let me down.

    | | F
You have found her, now go and get her.

 | B♭ | F
Re - member to let her into your heart,

     | C7 | F |
Then you can start to make it bet - ter.

Bridge 2

F7   ‖Bb
So let it out and let it in,

     Bbmaj7 |Bb6
Hey Jude, be - gin,

            |Bb |C7 |F |
You're wait - ing for some - one to per - form with.

F7 |Bb
And don't you know that it's just you?

    Bbmaj7 |Bb6
Hey Jude, you'll do.

   Bb |C7 |F
The movement you need is on your should - er.

     |F7   C7 | |
Na, na, na, na, na, na, na, na, na. Yeah.

Verse 4

  ‖F |C7
Hey Jude, don't make it bad.

  | |F
Take a sad song and make it better.

 |Bb |F
Re - member to let her under your skin,

      |C7 |F |
Then you be - gin to make it bet - ter,

      | ‖
Better, better, better, better, better, oh.

Outro

‖: F |Eb |
  Na,   na, na, na, na, na, na,

Bb |F   :‖ *Repeat and fade*
Na, na, na, na.   Hey Jude.

Let It Be

Words and Music by
John Lennon and Paul McCartney

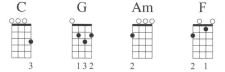

Intro

|C   G |Am   F |C   G |F   C

Verse 1

‖C   G |
When I find myself in times of trouble

Am   F |
Mother Mary comes to me

C   G
Speaking words of wis - dom,

   |F   C
Let it be.

   | G
And in my hour of dark - ness

   |Am   F |
She is standing right in front of me

C   G
Speaking words of wisdom,

   |F   C
Let it be.

Chorus 1

‖Am   G
Let it be, __ let it be,

        |F   C |
Ah, let it be, __ let it be.

                    G
Whisper words of wisdom,

   |F   C
Let it be.

Verse 2

```
 ‖C                        G            |
And when the broken heart - ed people
Am              F          |
Living in the world __ agree,
C              G
There will be an an - swer,
    |F    C
Let it be.
    |                      G            |
For though they may be part - ed there is
Am                    F          |
Still a chance that they __ will see
C              G
There will be an an - swer,
    |F    C
Let it be.
```

Chorus 2

```
         ‖Am        G
Let it be, __ let it be,
         |F          C
Ah, let it be, __ let it be.
    |                  G
Yeah, there will be an an - swer,
    |F    C
Let it be.
```

Chorus 3   *Repeat Chorus 1*

Interlude   F   C |G   F   C |F   C |G   F   C ‖

Guitar Solo   C   G |Am   F |C   G |F   C |
                          G |Am   F |C   G |F   C

Chorus 4   *Repeat Chorus 1*

Verse 3

```
        ‖C                    G
        And when the night is cloud - y
           |Am          F              |
        There is still a light that shines on me;
        C           G
        Shine until tomor - row,
            |F    C
        Let it be.
        |                    G              |
        I wake up to the sound __ of music;
        Am                   F         |
        Mother Mary comes __ to me,
        C                G
        Speaking words of wisdom,
            |F    C
        Let it be.
```

Chorus 5

```
           ‖Am          G
        Let it be, __ let it be,
                    |F          C
        Ah, let it be, __ let it be.
             |                  G
        Yeah, there will be an an - swer,
            |F    C
        Let it be.
             |Am          G
        Let it be, __ let it be,
                    |F          C   |
        Ah, let it be, __ let it be.
                         G
        Whisper words of wisdom,
            |F    C  |F    C  |G   F   C  ‖
        Let it be.
```

I Saw Her Standing There

Words and Music by
John Lennon and Paul McCartney

E7   A7   B7   E   C

Intro

N.C. |E7 | | |
One, two, three, four!

Verse 1

                    ‖ E7 |
Well, she was just   seventeen,

    |A7 |E7
You know what I mean,

    | | |B7 |
And the way she looked was way beyond com - pare.

    |E |E7 |A7 |C
So how could I dance   with anoth - er,   woo,

    |E7 |B7 |E7 |
When I saw   her   standing there?

Verse 2

                    ‖ E7 |
Well, she   looked at me,

    |A7 |E7
And I,   I could see

    | | |B7 | |
That be - fore too long I'd   fall in love with her.

    E |E7 |A7 |C
She wouldn't dance   with anoth - er,   woo,

    |E7 |B7 |E7 |
When I saw   her   standing there.

Bridge 1

```
   ‖A7                      |
Well, my heart went boom
   |                    |
When I crossed that room
   |            |       |B7      |      |A7       |
And I held her hand     in    mine.
```

Verse 3

```
                  ‖ E7                  |
Oh, we danced      through the night,
        |A7               |E7
And we held each other tight,
        |            |            |B7         |
And be - fore too long I  fell in love with her.
     |E            |E7          |A7           |C
Now I'll never dance     with anoth - er,     woo,
     |E7        |B7          |E7        |        ‖
Since I saw   her   standing there.
```

Interlude

```
E7      |      |      |      |      |B7      |      |
E    |E7    |A7    |    |E7    |B7    |E7    ‖
```

Bridge 2

Repeat Bridge 1

Verse 4

```
                  ‖ E7                  |
Oh, we danced      through the night,
        |A7               |E7
And we held each other tight,
        |            |            |B7         |
And be - fore too long I  fell in love with her.
     |E            |E7          |A7           |C
Now I'll never dance     with anoth - er,     woo,
        |E7        |B7          |E7        |
Since I saw   her   standing there.
E7             |         |B7          |E7        |
   Oh, since I saw   her     standing there.
              |E7        |B7          |A7    |E7      |          ‖
Yeah, well, since I saw   her     standing there.
```

I Want to Hold Your Hand

Words and Music by
John Lennon and Paul McCartney

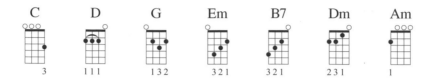

Intro

C D | C D | C D | |

Verse 1

‖G |D |
Oh yeah, I tell you something,

Em |B7
I think you'll under - stand.

|G |D |
When I say that something,

Em |B7 ‖
I wanna hold your hand.

Chorus 1

C D |G Em |
I wanna hold your hand,

C D |G
I wanna hold your hand.

Verse 2

‖G |D |
Oh please, say to me

Em |B7
You'll let me be your man.

|G |D |
And please say to me

Em |B7 ‖
You'll let me hold your hand.

Chorus 2

C D |G Em |
Now let me hold your hand,

C D |G ‖
I wanna hold your hand.

Bridge 1

Dm |G
And when I touch you
    |C |Am |
I feel happy in - side.
Dm |G
It's such a feeling
      |C |D
That my love I can't hide,
C |D   C |D |
I can't hide, I can't hide.

Verse 3

      ‖G |D |
Yeah, you got that something,
Em |B7
I think you'll under - stand.
  |G |D |
When I say that something,
Em |B7   ‖
I wanna hold your hand.

Chorus 3   *Repeat Chorus 1*

Bridge 2   *Repeat Bridge 1*

Verse 4

      ‖G |D |
Yeah, you got that something,
Em |B7
I think you'll under - stand.
  |G |D |
When I feel that something,
Em |B7   ‖
I wanna hold your hand.

Chorus 4

C   D |G Em |
I wanna hold your hand.
C   D |B7 |
I wanna hold your hand.
C   D |C |G   ‖
I wanna hold your hand.

I Will

Words and Music by
John Lennon and Paul McCartney

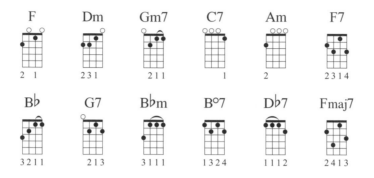

Verse 1

‖**F**   **Dm** |**Gm7** **C7**
Who knows how long I've loved you?

|**F**   **Dm** |**Am**
You know I love you still.

F7 |**B♭**   **C7** |**Dm**   **F**
Will I wait a lonely lifetime?

|**B♭**   **C7** |**F** **Dm** |**Gm7** **C7**
If you want me to, I will.

Verse 2

‖**F** **Dm** |**Gm7** **C7**
For if I ever saw you,

|**F** **Dm** |**Am**
I didn't catch your name.

F7 |**B♭** **C7** |**Dm**   **F**
But it never really mattered;

|**B♭** **C7** |**F**   **F7** ‖
I will always feel the same.

Bridge

B♭   **Am** | **Dm** |
Love you for - ever   and forever,

Gm7   **C7** | **F**   **F7** |
Love you with all my heart.

B♭   **Am** | **Dm** |
Love you when - ever we're together,

G7 | **C7**
Love you when we're a - part.

Verse 3

   ‖ **F**   **Dm** | **Gm7**   **C7**
And when at last I find you,

  | **F**   **Dm** | **Am**
Your song will fill the air.

F7 | **B♭**   **C7** | **Dm**   **B♭m**   **F**
Sing it loud so I can hear you.

       | **B♭**   **C7** | **Dm**   **B♭m**   **F**
Make it easy to be near you.

      | **B♭**   **C7**
For the things you do

     | **Dm**   **B♭m**   **F**   **B°7** |
En - dear you   to me,

Gm7   **C7** | **D♭7** |
Ah, you know I will,

     | **F** | **F7**   ‖
I will.

Outro   **B♭**   **Am** | **Dm** | **Gm7**   **C7** | **Fmaj7**   ‖

I'll Follow the Sun

Words and Music by
John Lennon and Paul McCartney

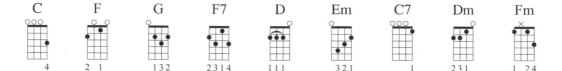

Intro

　　　　　　　C　　　|F　　C　　‖

Verse 1

　　　　　　　G　　|F7　　　　　|
　　　　　　　One day you'll look
　　　　　　　C　　　　|D
　　　　　　　　To see I've gone,
　　　　　　　　　|C　　　　Em　　　|
　　　　　　　For tomorrow may rain, so
　　　　　　　D　　G　　　|C　|F　C　‖
　　　　　　　　I'll follow the sun.

Verse 2

　　　　　　　G　　|F7　　　　　|
　　　　　　　Some day you'll know
　　　　　　　C　　　　|D
　　　　　　　　I was the one,
　　　　　　　　　|C　　　　Em　　　|
　　　　　　　But tomorrow may rain, so
　　　　　　　D　　G　　　|C　|C7
　　　　　　　　I'll follow the sun.

Bridge 1

‖ **Dm**
And now the time has come,

|**Fm** |**C** |
And so, my love, I must go.

C7 |**Dm** |
And though I lose a friend

Fm |**C** |**Dm**   ‖
In the end you will know, oh.

Verse 3

G |**F7** |
One day you'll find

C |**D**
  That I have gone,

   |**C**   **Em** |
But tomorrow may rain, so

D   **G** |**C** |**F**   **C** ‖
  I'll follow the sun.

Solo

G |**F7** |**C** |

D |**C**   **Em** |
  Yes, tomorrow may rain, so

D   **G** |**C** |**C7**
  I'll follow the sun.

Bridge 2   *Repeat Bridge 1*

Verse 4

G |**F7** |
One day you'll find

C |**D**
  That I have gone,

   |**C**   **Em** |
But tomorrow may rain, so

D   **G** |**C** |**F**   **C** ‖
  I'll follow the sun.

If I Fell

Words and Music by
John Lennon and Paul McCartney

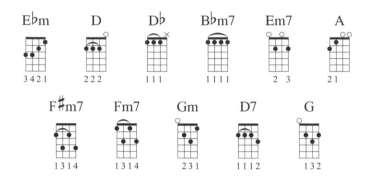

Intro

‖**E♭m**
If I fell in love with you,

　　　　　|**D**
Would you promise to be true

　　　|**D♭**　　　**B♭m7**
And help me understand?

　　　　　|**E♭m**
'Cause I've been in love before,

　　　|**D**
And I found that love was more

|**Em7**　　　　|**A**
Than just holding hands.

Verse 1

　　　　　‖**D　Em7** |**F♯m7　Fm7** |**Em7**
If I give my　　heart　to　　　you,

|**A**
I must be sure

　　　　　|**D　Em7** |**F♯m7　Fm7** |**Em7**
From the ve - ry　　start,　that　　you

　　　|**A**　　　　　　　　|**D**　　|**Gm　A**
Would love me more than her.

Verse 2

```
    ‖ D    Em7 |F♯m7  Fm7 |Em7
If I trust in     you,   oh     please,
      |A
Don't run and hide.
      |D    Em7 |F♯m7  Fm7 |Em7
If I love you   too,    oh     please,
      |A                      |D7
Don't hurt my pride like her.
```

Bridge 1

```
         ‖ D7                |G
'Cause I couldn't stand the pain.
      |Gm           |        |D
And I would be sad if our new love
      |A
Was in vain.
```

Verse 3

```
      ‖ D    Em7 |F♯m7  Fm7  |Em7
So I hope you    see     that    I
      |A                  |
Would love to love you.
 D   Em7 |F♯m7  Fm7  |Em7
And that  she     will    cry
      |A                      |D7
When she learns we are two.
```

Bridge 2

Repeat Bridge 1

Verse 4

```
      ‖ D    Em7 |F♯m7  Fm7  |Em7
So I hope you    see     that    I
      |A                  |
Would love to love you.
 D   Em7 |F♯m7  Fm7  |Em7
And that  she     will    cry
      |A             |D
When she learns we are two.
      |Gm           |D   |Gm   |D    ‖
If I fell in love with you.
```

Lady Madonna

Words and Music by
John Lennon and Paul McCartney

Intro   A   D |A   D |A   D |F   G   A ‖

Verse 1

    A   D |A   D |
Lady Ma - donna, children at your feet.

    A   D |F G   A |
Wonder how you manage to make ends meet.

              D |A   D |
Who finds the money when you pay the rent?

    A   D |F   G   A ‖
Did you think that money was heav - en sent?

Bridge 1

Dm |G |
Friday night arrives without a suitcase,

C |Am |
Sunday morning, creeping like a nun.

Dm |G |
Monday's child has learned to tie his bootlace.

C Bm7 |E7sus4 E7 ‖
See how they run.

	A D |A D |
Verse 2	Lady Ma - donna, baby at your breast.
	A D |F G A |
	Wonders how you manage to feed the rest.

Interlude 1   A   D |A   D |A   D |F   G   A ||

Solo   Dm |G |C |Am |Dm |G |

C Bm7 |E7sus4 E7 ||
See how they run.

	A D |A D |
Verse 3	Lady Ma - donna, lying on the bed.
	A D |F G A ||
	Listen to the music playing in your head.

Interlude 2   *Repeat Interlude 1*

	Dm |G |
Bridge 2	Tuesday afternoon is never - ending.
	C |Am |
	Wednesday morning, papers didn't come.
	Dm |G |
	Thursday night, your stockings needed mending.
	C Bm7 |E7sus4 E7 ||
	See how they run.

	A D |A D |
Verse 4	Lady Ma - donna, children at your feet.
	A D |F G |A Bm7 |Cm6 Bm7 A ||
	Wonder how you manage to make ends meet.

Outro |A   Bm7 |Cm6 Bm7 A ||

The Long and Winding Road

Words and Music by
John Lennon and Paul McCartney

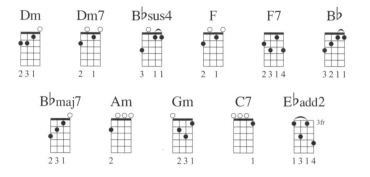

Verse 1

‖ **Dm**   **Dm7** |**B♭sus4**
The long and winding road

   |**F**   **F7** |**B♭** **B♭maj7** |
That leads to your door

B♭   **Am** |**Dm** **Dm7** |
   Will never disap - pear.

Gm   **C7** |**E♭add2** **F** |
   I've seen that road be - fore.

B♭ **Am** |**Dm**   **Dm7** |
   It always leads me here,

Gm   **C7** |**F**
   Lead me to your door.

Verse 2

‖ **Dm**   **Dm7** |**B♭sus4**
The wild and windy night

      |**F** **F7** |**B♭** **B♭maj7** |
That the rain washed a - way,

B♭   **Am** |**Dm** **Dm7** |
   Has left a   pool of tears

Gm   **C7** |**E♭add2** **F** |
   Crying for the day.

B♭   **Am** |**Dm** **Dm7** |
   Why leave me stand - ing   here?

Gm   **C7** |**F**   ‖
Let me know the way.

Bridge

F   B♭
Many times I've been alone,
  |F   Gm C7 |
And many times I've cried.
F   B♭
Anyway, you'll never know
  |F   Gm   C7
The many ways I've tried.

Verse 3

    ‖ Dm   Dm7 |B♭sus4
And still they lead me back
        |F F7 |B♭ B♭maj7 |
To the long, winding road.
B♭ Am |Dm Dm7 |
  You left me stand - ing here
Gm   C7 |E♭add2 F |
  A long, long time ago.
B♭ Am |Dm Dm7 |
  Don't leave me wait - ing here,
Gm   C7 |F   ‖
  Lead me to your door.

Interlude

‖:F B♭ |F Gm C7 :‖

Verse 4

    ‖ Dm   Dm7 |B♭sus4
But still they lead me back
        |F F7 |B♭ B♭maj7 |
To the long, winding road.
B♭ Am |Dm Dm7 |
  You left me standing here
Gm   C7 |E♭add2 F |
  A long, long time ago.
B♭ Am |Dm Dm7 |
  Don't keep me wait - ing here,
Gm   C7 |F |
  Lead me to your ___ door.
B♭sus4   F | | ‖
  Yeah, yeah, yeah, yeah.

Love Me Do

Words and Music by
John Lennon and Paul McCartney

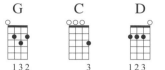

Intro

G |C |G |C |

G |C |G | ||

Chorus 1

G |C
Love, love me do.

  |G |C
You know I love you.

  |G |C
I'll always be true.

| | |
So please,

N.C. |G |C |G |C ||
Love me do.   Oh, love me do.

Chorus 2

G |C
Love, love me do.

  |G |C
You know I love you.

  |G |C
I'll always be true.

| | |
So please,

N.C. |G |C |G | ||
Love me do.   Oh, love me do.

Bridge

D | |
Someone to love,
C |**G** |
Somebody new.
D | |
Someone to love,
C |**G** ||
Someone like you.

Chorus 3

Repeat Chorus 2

Solo

‖:**D** | |**C** |**G** :‖
| | | **N.C.** ‖

Chorus 4

G |**C**
Love, love me do.
|**G** |**C**
You know I love you.
|**G** |**C**
I'll always be true.
| | |
So please,
N.C. |**G** |**C** |**G** |**C**
Love me do. Oh, love me do.
‖:**G** |**C**
Yeah, love me do.
|**G** |**C** :‖ *Repeat and fade*
Oh, love me do. Yeah,

Lucy in the Sky with Diamonds

Words and Music by
John Lennon and Paul McCartney

A5   A7*   F#m7   Dm*   A   A7   A6   F6

F   Dm   Dm7   Bb   Cadd9   G   D   C

Intro

A5 |A7* |F#m7 |Dm*   ‖

Verse 1

A |A7 |A6 |F6
Picture your - self in a boat on a river,

|A |A7 |A6 |F | |
With tangerine trees and marmalade skies.

A |A7 |A6 |F6
Somebody calls you, you answer quite slowly,

|A |A7 |A6 | |Dm |Dm7   ‖
A girl with ka - leidoscope eyes.

Pre-Chorus 1

Bb | |Cadd9 | |
Cellophane flowers of yellow and green,

F6 | |Bb | |
Towering over your head.

Cadd9 | |G |
Look for the girl with the sun in her eyes,

|D   ‖
And she's gone.

Chorus 1

G   C |D |
Lucy in the sky with diamonds.

G   C |D |
Lucy in the sky with diamonds.

G   C |D |
Lucy in the sky with diamonds.

‖
Ah.

Verse 2

```
A          |A7        |A6         |F6
Follow her down to a bridge by a fountain,
     |A          |A7        |A6         |F       |       |
Where rocking horse people eat marshmallow pies.
A          |A7        |A6         |F6
Everyone smiles as you drift past the flowers,
     |A          |A7        |A6      |       |Dm      |Dm7      ||
That grow so in - credibly high.
```

Pre-Chorus 2

```
B♭          |        |Cadd9      |       |
Newspaper tax - is ap - pear on the shore,
F6          |        |B♭       |       |
Waiting to take you a - way.
Cadd9          |        |G       |
Climb in the back with your head in the clouds,
          |D        ||
And you're gone.
```

Chorus 2   *Repeat Chorus 1*

Verse 3

```
A              |A7        |A6         |F6
Picture your - self on a train in a station,
     |A          |A7        |A6         |F       |       |
With plasticine porters with looking glass ties.
A          |A7        |A6         |F6
Suddenly someone is there at the turnstile,
     |A          |A7        |A6      |       |Dm7      ||
The girl with ka - leidoscope eyes.
```

Chorus 3

```
‖: G          C          |D          |
   Lucy in the sky with diamonds.
G          C          |D          |
Lucy in the sky with diamonds.
G          C          |D          |
Lucy in the sky with diamonds.
          |A      :‖ Repeat and fade
Ah.
```

Michelle

Words and Music by
John Lennon and Paul McCartney

Fm   Fm(maj7)   Fm7   Fm6   B♭m   B♭m(add9)   B♭m7   C5   F

B♭7♯9   E6   D°7   C   B°7   Fm*   A♭7   D♭

Intro

|Fm Fm(maj7) |Fm7 Fm6 |

|B♭m B♭m(add9) B♭m B♭m7 |C5   ‖

Verse 1

|F |B♭7♯9 |
Michelle, ma belle.

|E♭6 |D°7 |C
These are words that go together well,

B°7 |C   ‖
My Mi - chelle.

Verse 2

|F |B♭7♯9 |
Michelle, ma belle.

|E♭6 |D°7 |C
Sont les mots qui vont très bien en - semble,

B°7 |C
Très bien en - semble.

Bridge 1

‖Fm* | |
I love you, I love you, I love you.

|A♭7 |D♭ |
That's all I want to say.

|C |Fm*
Until I find a way,

|Fm Fm(maj7) |Fm7 Fm6
I will say the only   words I know

|B♭m B♭m(add9) B♭m B♭m7 |C5   ‖
That you'll   un - der - stand.

Verse 3

Repeat Verse 2

Bridge 2

```
‖Fm*                    |              |
 I need to, I need to, I need to,
A♭7                 |D♭        |
  I need to make you see,
C                       |Fm*
  Oh, what you mean to me.
      |Fm  Fm(maj7) |Fm7    Fm6
Until I  do I'm         hoping you
     |B♭m  B♭m(add9)  B♭m   B♭m7 |C5          ‖
Will know            what   I       mean.
```

Solo

```
|Fm*         |B♭7♯9  |
  I love you.
|E♭6  |D°7    |C  B°7  |C
```

Bridge 3

```
‖Fm*                   |              |
 I want you, I want you, I want you.
A♭7                |D♭        |
  I think you know by now,
C                       |Fm*
  I'll get to you some - how.
      |Fm   Fm(maj7) |Fm7    Fm6
Un - til  I  do   I'm      telling you,
     |B♭m  Bm(add9)  B♭m   B♭m7 |C5          ‖
So you'll              un - der - stand.
```

Verse 4

```
|F         |B♭7♯9   |
 Michelle,   ma belle.
|E♭6             |D°7              |C
 Sont les mots qui vont très bien en - semble,
B°7           |C
Très bien en - semble.
        |Fm      Fm(maj7) |Fm7       Fm6
And I will say the only        words I know
    |B♭m  B♭m(add9)  B♭m   B♭m7 |C5             |
That you'll            un - der - stand, my Michelle.
```

Outro

```
‖:F         |B♭7♯9    |E♭6        |
|D°7         |C  B°7   |C            :‖  Repeat & fade
```

Norwegian Wood
(This Bird Has Flown)

Words and Music by
John Lennon and Paul McCartney

F   F6   B♭sus2   F*   C5   C7

C6   E♭   B♭   Fm   Gm   C

Intro

‖: F   F6   F   B♭sus2 | F*   C5   C7   C6 |
    F*   E♭   B♭ | F*   :‖

Verse 1

F |
I once had a girl,

         |
Or should I say

E♭   B♭ | F* |
She once had   me?

F |
She showed me her room,

         |
Isn't it good,

E♭   B♭ | F*
Norwe - gian   wood?

Bridge 1

‖ Fm | | B♭ |
She asked me to stay and she told me to sit anywhere.

| Fm | | Gm | C   ‖
So I looked around and I noticed there wasn't a chair.

Verse 2

```
|F          |
 I sat on a rug

            |
Biding my time,
Eb      Bb  |F*     |
Drinking her   wine.
F           |
We talked until two,

            |
And then she said,
 Eb      Bb  |F*        ||
"It's time for    bed."
```

Interlude

```
||:F      F6  F  Bbsus2 |F*    C5  C7  C6  |
  F*      Eb      Bb  |F*              :||
```

Bridge 2

```
    ||Fm                    |               |Bb      |
She told me she worked in the morn - ing and started to laugh.
  |Fm            |                    |Gm    |C      ||
I   told her I didn't and crawled off to sleep in the bath.
```

Verse 3

```
F           |
And when I a - woke

            |
I was a - lone,
Eb      Bb  |F*     |
This bird had   flown.
F       |
So I lit a fire,

            |
Isn't it good,
Eb      Bb  |F*        ||
Norwe - gian   wood?
```

Outro

```
F       F6  F  Bbsus2 |F*    C5  C7  C6  |
F*      Eb      Bb  |F*              ||
```

Nowhere Man

Words and Music by
John Lennon and Paul McCartney

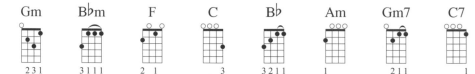

Verse 1

N.C.(**F**) | |
He's a real nowhere man,

| |
Sitting in his nowhere land,
Gm |**B♭m** |**F** | ||
Making all his nowhere plans for nobody.

Verse 2

F |**C** |
Doesn't have a point of view.
B♭ |**F** |
Knows not where he's going to.
Gm |**B♭m** |**F** |
Isn't he a bit like you and me?

Bridge 1

||**Am** |**B♭**
Nowhere man, please listen.
|**Am** |**B♭**
You don't know what you're missing.
|**Am** |**Gm7** | |**C7** ||
Nowhere man, the world is at your command.

Solo   F |C |B♭ |F |
                            Gm7 |B♭m |F | ‖

Verse 3   F |C |
                            He's as blind as he can be.
                            B♭ |F |
                            Just sees what he wants to see.
                            Gm |B♭m |F |
                            Nowhere man, can you see me at all?

Bridge 2   ‖Am |B♭
                            Nowhere man, don't worry.
                                 |Am |B♭
                            Take your time, don't hurry.
                                 |Am |Gm7 | |C7   ‖
                            Leave it all till somebody else lends you a hand.

Verse 4   *Repeat Verse 2*

Bridge 3   *Repeat Bridge 1*

Verse 5   F |C |
                            He's a real nowhere man,
                            B♭ |F |
                            Sitting in his nowhere land,
                            Gm |B♭m |F | |
                            Making all his nowhere plans for nobody.
                            Gm |B♭m |F | |
                            Making all his nowhere plans for nobody.
                            Gm |B♭m |F | ‖
                            Making all his nowhere plans for nobody.

Ob-La-Di, Ob-La-Da

Words and Music by
John Lennon and Paul McCartney

Bb   F   F7   Eb   Dm   Gm   Bbsus2   Bb7

Intro

Bb | | | ||

Verse 1

Bb |F |
Desmond has a barrow in the market place,
F7 |Bb |
Molly is the singer in a band.
                              |Eb
Desmond says to Molly, girl, I like your face,
      |Bb   F |Bb
And Molly says this as she takes him by the hand.

Chorus 1

     ||Bb |Dm Gm |
Ob-la-di, ob-la-da, life goes on,   bra,
Bb   F |Bb
La, la, how their life goes on.
            | |Dm Gm |
Ob-la-di, ob-la-da, life goes on,   bra,
Bb |F |Bb ||
La, la, how their life goes on.

Verse 2

Bb |F |
Desmond takes a trolley to the jeweler's store,
F7 |Bb |
Buys a twenty carat golden ring.
                              |Eb
Takes it back to Molly waiting at the door,
        |Bb   F |Bb
And as he gives it to her, she begins to sing:

Chorus 2

Repeat Chorus 1

Bridge 1

Eb
  In a couple of years,
         | |Bb Bbsus2 |Bb Bb7 |
They have built a home sweet home.
Eb |
  With a couple of kids running in the yard
 |Bb |F7 ||
Of Desmond and Molly Jones.

Verse 3

Bb |F |
Happy ever after in the market place,
F7 |Bb |
Desmond lets the children lend a hand.
                      |Eb
Molly stays at home and does her pretty face,
      |Bb   F |Bb
And in the evening she still sings it with the band.

Chorus 3   *Repeat Chorus 1*

Bridge 2   *Repeat Bridge 1*

Verse 4

Bb |F |
Happy ever after in the market place,
F7 |Bb |
Molly lets the children lend a hand.
                      |Eb
Desmond stays at home and does his pretty face,
      |Bb   F |Bb
And in the evening she's a singer with the band.

Chorus 4

        ||Bb |Dm Gm |
Ob-la-di, ob-la-da, life goes on, bra,
Bb   F |Bb
La, la, how their life goes on.
           | |Dm Gm |
Ob-la-di, ob-la-da, life goes on, bra,
Bb |F |Gm
La, la, how their life goes on.

          |
And if you want some fun,
   |F   Bb ||
Take ob-la-di-bla-da.

Penny Lane

Words and Music by
John Lennon and Paul McCartney

B   C#m7   F#7   Bm7   G#m7b5

3 2 1 1   3 3 3 3   2 3 1 4   1 1 1 1   1 3 3 3

Gmaj7   F#7sus4   E   A   D

1 1 1   2 3 1 4   2 3 4 1   2 1   2 3 4

Verse 1

‖**B** |**C#m7**   **F#7**
Penny Lane there is a barber showing photographs
 |**B** |**Bm7**
Of ev'ry head he's had the pleasure to know.
 |**G#m7b5** |**Gmaj7**
And all the people that come and go,
 |**F#7sus4**   **F#7** |**F#7sus4**   **F#7**
Stop and say hello.

Verse 2

‖**B** |**C#m7**   **F#7**
On the corner is a banker with a motorcar,
 |**B** |**Bm7**
The little children laugh at him behind his back.
 |**G#m7b5** |**Gmaj7**
And the banker never wears a mac
 |**F#7sus4**   **F#7** |**E**
In the pouring rain.   Very strange.

Chorus 1

‖**A** | |**D** | |
Penny Lane is in my ears and in my eyes.
A | |**D**
There beneath the blue suburban skies
 |**F#7**
I sit, and meanwhile back…

Verse 3

‖B |C♯m7 F♯7
In Penny Lane there is a fireman with an hourglass,

|B |Bm7
And in his pocket is a portrait of the Queen.

|G♯m7♭5 |Gmaj7
He likes to keep his fire engine clean.

|F♯7sus4 F♯7 |F♯7sus4 F♯7 ‖
It's a clean machine.

Solo

B |C♯m7 F♯7 |B |Bm7 |
G♯m7♭5 |Gmaj7 |F♯7sus4 F♯7 |E

Chorus 2

‖A | |D | |
Penny Lane is in my ears and in my eyes.

A | |D
 A four of fish and finger pies

|F♯7
In summer, meanwhile back…

Verse 4

‖B |C♯m7 F♯7
Behind the shelter in the middle of the roundabout

|B |Bm7
The pretty nurse is selling poppies from a tray.

|G♯m7♭5 |Gmaj7
And though she feels as if she's in a play,

|F♯7sus4 F♯7 |F♯7sus4 F♯7
She is anyway.

Verse 5

```
              ‖B                           |C♯m7      F♯7
In Penny Lane the barber shaves another customer.
        |B                    |Bm7
We see the banker sitting waiting for a trim.
          |G♯m7♭5      |Gmaj7
And then the fireman rushes in
        |F♯7sus4      F♯7 |E
From the pouring rain.      Very strange.
```

Chorus 3

```
          ‖A            |              |D        |          |
Penny Lane is in my ears and in my eyes.
A               |              |D
There beneath the blue suburban skies
        |F♯7
I sit, and meanwhile back…
        |B            |              |E        |          |
Penny Lane is in my ears and in my eyes.
B               |              |E        |
There beneath the blue suburban skies…
              |B        ‖
Penny Lane.
```

She Loves You

Words and Music by
John Lennon and Paul McCartney

Em   A   C   G   Bm   D   Cm   Em6   C*   G6

Chorus 1

‖**Em** |
She loves you, yeah,   yeah, yeah.

|**A** |
She loves you, yeah,   yeah, yeah.

|**C** | |**G** |
She loves you, yeah,   yeah, yeah,   yeah.

Verse 1

‖**G** |**Em**
You think you lost your love?

|**Bm** |**D**
Well, I saw her yester - day.

|**G** |**Em**
It's you she's thinking of

|**Bm** |**D**
And she told me what to say:

Pre-Chorus 1

‖**G**
She says she loves you

| |**Em** |
And you know that can't be bad.

|**Cm**
Yes, she loves you

| |**D** |
And you know you should be glad.

Verse 2

```
    ‖G                        |Em
She said you hurt her so,
    |Bm              |D
She almost lost her mind.
    |G                        |Em
But now she said she knows
      |Bm              |D
You're not the hurting kind.
```

Pre-Chorus 2

```
                    ‖G
She says she loves you
      |                    |Em            |
And you know that can't be bad.
        |Cm
Yes, she loves you
      |                        |D              |
And you know you should be glad,          ooh!
```

Chorus 2

```
    ‖Em              |
She loves you, yeah,  yeah, yeah.
    |A              |
She loves you, yeah,  yeah, yeah.
          |Cm
And with a love like that
    |D                        |G              |
You know you should be glad.
```

Verse 3

```
    ‖G                        |Em
You know it's up to you;
    |Bm              |D          |
I think it's only fair.
G                        |Em
Pride can hurt you too;
    |Bm          |D
A - pologize to her
```

Pre-Chorus 3

‖**G**
Because she loves you

| |**Em** |
And you know that can't be bad.

|**Cm**
Yes, she loves you

| |**D**
And you know you should be glad,   ooh!

Chorus 3

‖**Em** |
She loves you, yeah, yeah, yeah.

|**A** |
She loves you, yeah, yeah, yeah.

|**Cm**
And with a love like that

|**D** |**G** |**Em**
You know you should be glad.

|**Cm**
With a love like that

|**D** |**G** |**Em**
You know you should be glad.

|**Cm**
With a love like that,

Outro

|**D** ‖**G**
You know you should be glad.

|**Em6** | |
   Yeah, yeah, yeah.

|**C*** | |**G6** ‖
   Yeah, yeah, yeah, yeah!

Something

Words and Music by
George Harrison

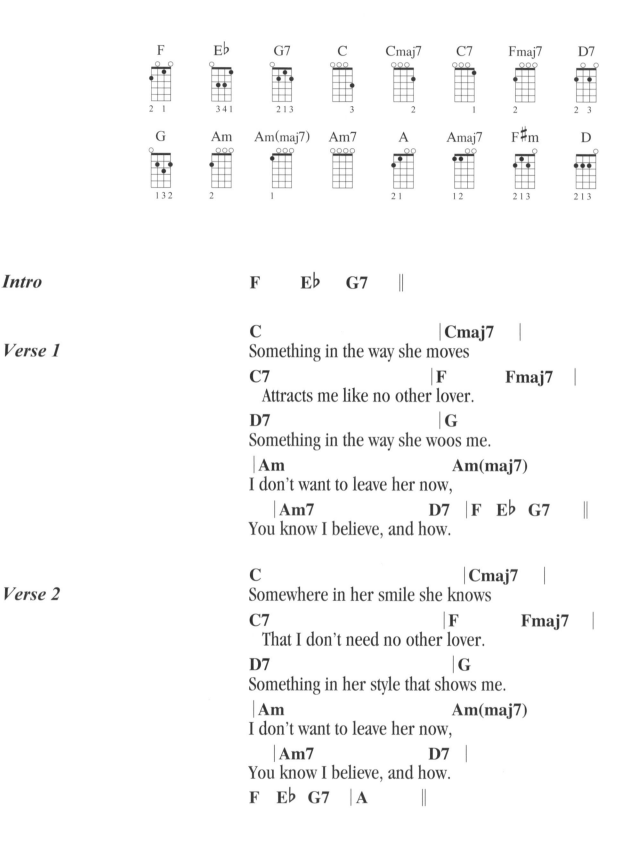

Intro   F   E♭   G7   ‖

Verse 1

C |Cmaj7 |
Something in the way she moves
C7 |F   Fmaj7 |
 Attracts me like no other lover.
D7 |G
Something in the way she woos me.
|Am   Am(maj7)
I don't want to leave her now,
    |Am7   D7 |F E♭ G7   ‖
You know I believe, and how.

Verse 2

C |Cmaj7 |
Somewhere in her smile she knows
C7 |F   Fmaj7 |
 That I don't need no other lover.
D7 |G
Something in her style that shows me.
|Am   Am(maj7)
I don't want to leave her now,
    |Am7   D7 |
You know I believe, and how.
F E♭ G7 |A   ‖

Bridge

<pre>
A   Amaj7 |F♯m   A
   You're asking me will my love grow,
    |D   G |A |
I don't know, I don't know.
            Amaj7 |F♯m   A
You stick around now, it may show,
    |D   G |C   ‖
I don't know, I don't know.
</pre>

Interlude

<pre>
C |Cmaj7 |C7 |F Fmaj7 |D7 |G |
Am Am(maj7) |Am7   D7 |F   E♭ G7   ‖
</pre>

Verse 3

<pre>
C |Cmaj7 |
Something in the way she knows,
C7 |F   Fmaj7 |
   And all I have to do is think of her.
D7 |G
Something in the things she shows me.
 |Am   Am(maj7)
I don't want to leave her now,
    |Am7   D7   ‖
You know I believe, and how.
</pre>

Outro

<pre>
F E♭ G7 |A |F E♭ G7 |C   ‖
</pre>

Ticket to Ride

Words and Music by
John Lennon and Paul McCartney

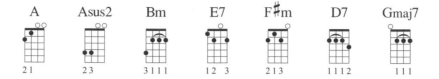

Intro   A   Asus2 |A   Asus2 |A   Asus2 |A   Asus2

Verse 1

‖A |
I think I'm gonna be sad;

                     | |
I think it's today,   yeah.

          | |
The girl that's driving me mad

                    |Bm |E7   ‖
Is going away.

Chorus 1

F#m |D7 |
She's got a ticket to ride,
F#m |Gmaj7 |
She's got a ticket to ri - hi-hide,
F#m |E7
She's got a ticket to ride,

                    |A   Asus2 |A   Asus2
And she don't care.

Verse 2

‖A |
She said that living with me

                     | | |
Was bringing her down,   yeah.

                    |
She would never be free

                    |Bm |E7   ‖
When I was around.

Chorus 2   *Repeat Chorus 1*

Bridge 1

‖**D7** |
I don't know why she's ridin' so high.

| |**E7**
She ought to think twice, she ought to do right by me.
|**D7** |
Be - fore she gets to sayin' goodbye,

| |**E7** |
She ought to think twice, she ought to do right by me.

Verse 3   *Repeat Verse 1*

Chorus 3   *Repeat Chorus 1*

Bridge 2   *Repeat Bridge 1*

Verse 4   *Repeat Verse 2*

Chorus 4

F#m |**D7** |
She's got a ticket to ride,
F#m |**Gmaj7** |
She's got a ticket to ri   -   hi-hide,
F#m |**E7**
She's got a ticket to ride,

|**A**   **Asus2** |**A**
And she don't care.

Outro

N.C.   ‖**A** |
My baby don't care.

| |
My baby don't care.

| |
My baby don't care.

| | ‖
My baby don't care.

With a Little Help from My Friends

Words and Music by
John Lennon and Paul McCartney

Chords: C, D, E, B, F#m7, B7, A, C#m7, F#

Intro

C | D | E | | ||
Bil - ly Shears.

Verse 1

E   B |F#m7
What would you think if I sang out of tune,
| B7 |E |
Would you stand up and walk out on me?
B |F#m7
Lend me your ears and I'll sing you a song,
| B7 |E
And I'll try not to sing out of key.

Chorus 1

||D   A |E
Oh, I get by with a little help from my friends.
|D   A |E
Mm, I get high with a little help from my friends.
|A |E |B | ||
Mm, I'm gonna try with a little help from my friends.

Verse 2

E   B |F#m7
What do I do when my love is away?
| B7 |E |
(Does it worry you to be a - lone?)
B |F#m7
How do I feel at the end of the day?
| B7 |E
(Are you sad because you're on your own?)

Chorus 2

‖D   A |E
No, I get by with a little help from my friends.

|D   A |E
Mm, I get high with a little help from my friends.

|A |E
Mm, gonna try with a little help from my friends.

Bridge 1

‖C♯m7 |F♯
(Do you need any - body?)

|E   D |A
I need some - body to love.

|C♯m7 |F♯
(Could it be any - body?)

|E   D |A   ‖
I want some - body to love.

Verse 3

E   B |F♯m7
(Would you be - lieve in a love at first sight?)

| B7 |E
Yes, I'm certain that it happens all the time.

B |F♯m7
(What do you see when you turn out the light?)

| B7 |E
I can't tell you, but I know it's mine.

Chorus 3

‖D   A |E
Oh, I get by with a little help from my friends.

|D   A |E
Mm, I get high with a little help from my friends.

|A |E
Oh, I'm gonna try with a little help from my friends.

Bridge 2

Repeat Bridge 1

Chorus 4

‖D   A |E
Oh, I get by with a little help from my friends.

|D   A |E
Mm, gonna try with a little help from my friends.

|A |E
Oh, I get high with a little help from my friends.

|D |A
Yes, I get by with a little help from my friends.

|C |D |E ‖
With a little help from my friends.

Yellow Submarine

Words and Music by
John Lennon and Paul McCartney

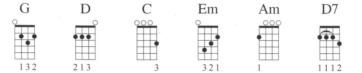

Verse 1

G   ‖D   C |G
In the town where I was born

Em |Am   C |D
Lived a man who sailed to sea.

G |D   C |G
And he told us of his life

Em |Am   C |D
In the land of subma - rines.

Verse 2

G   ‖D   C |G
So we sailed up to the sun

Em |Am   C |D
Till we found the sea of green.

G |D   C |G
And we lived be - neath the waves

Em |Am C |D   ‖
In our yellow subma - rine.

Chorus 1

G |D |
We all live in a yellow submarine,
         |G |
Yellow submarine, yellow submarine.
      |D |
We all live in a yellow submarine,
        |G
Yellow submarine, yellow submarine.

Verse 3

     ‖D   C |G
And our friends are all a - board,
Em |Am   C |D
Many more of them live next door.
G |D   C |G   Em |Am C |D7   G‖
And the band be - gins to play…

Chorus 2   *Repeat Chorus 1*

Interlude

D   C |G   Em |Am   C |D   G |
D   C |G   Em |Am   C |D

Verse 4

G ‖D   C |G
As we live a life of ease,
Em |Am   C |D
Every one of us has all we need:
G |D   C |G
Sky of blue and sea of green
Em |Am C |D   ‖
In our yellow subma - rine.

Outro   *Repeat Chorus 1*

Yesterday

Words and Music by
John Lennon and Paul McCartney

F   Em7   A7   Dm   Dm7   B♭maj7   C7

Fmaj7   Dm7*   G   B♭   Gm6   G7

Intro   **F** | ||

Verse 1

F |
Yesterday

Em7   **A7**   **|Dm**   **Dm7** |
   All my troubles seemed so far away.

B♭maj7   **C7**   **|F**
   Now it looks as though they're here to stay.

Fmaj7 **Dm7***   **G** **|B♭** **F** ||
Oh,   I believe   in yes - terday.

Verse 2

F |
Suddenly

Em7   **A7**   **|Dm**   **Dm7** |
   I'm not half the man I used to be.

B♭maj7   **C7**   **|F**
   There's a shadow hanging over me.

Fmaj7 **Dm7***   **G**   **|B♭** **F** ||
Oh,   yesterday   came sud - denly.

Bridge 1

Em7   A7 |Dm Dm7 B♭maj7
Why   she   had to   go

Dm7 |Gm6   C7 |F |
I   don't know, she wouldn't say.

Em7   A7 |Dm   Dm7 B♭maj7
I   said   some - thing wrong,

Dm7 |Gm6   C7 |F   ‖
Now I long for yester - day.

Verse 3

F |
Yesterday

Em7   A7 |Dm   Dm7 |
  Love was such an easy game to play.

B♭maj7   C7 |F
  Now I need a place to hide away.

Fmaj7 Dm7*   G |B♭ F   ‖
Oh,   I believe   in yes - terday.

Bridge 2   *Repeat Bridge 1*

Verse 4   *Repeat Verse 3*

F   G7 |B♭ F   ‖
Hmm._____

When I'm Sixty-Four

Words and Music by
John Lennon and Paul McCartney

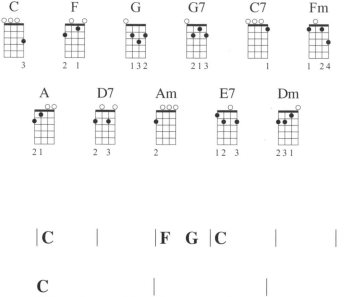

Intro |C | |F G |C | | ||

Verse 1
C | |
When I get older, losing my hair,
                        |G |
Many years from now,
G7   . | |
Will you still be sending me a valentine,
N.C. |C |
Birthday greetings, bottle of wine?
                 | |
If I'd been out till quarter to three,
C7 |F |
Would you lock the door?
                 Fm |C   A |
Will you still need me, will you still feed me,
D7   G7 |C G C ||
When I'm sixty-four?

Interlude   Am | |G |Am ||

Bridge 1

Am | |**E7** | |**Am** |
You'll be older too.

        |**Dm** | |
And if you say the word

F |**G** |**C** |**G** | ||
I could stay with you.

Verse 2

C | |
I could be handy, mending a fuse

        |**G** |
When your lights have gone.

G7 | |
You can knit a sweater by the fireside,

N.C. |**C** |
Sunday mornings, go for a ride.

    | |
Doing the garden, digging the weeds,

C7 |**F** |
Who could ask for more?

    Fm |**C**   **A** |
Will you still need me, will you still feed me

D7   **G7** |**C** **G** **C** ||
When I'm sixty-four?

Bridge 2

Am |
Every summer we can rent a cottage
    |**G** |**Am** |
In the Isle of Wight, if it's not too dear.
    | |**E7** | |**Am** |
We shall scrimp and save.
    |**Dm** | |
Grandchildren on your knee.
F |**G** |**C** |**G** | ‖
Vera, Chuck and Dave.

Verse 3

C | |
Send me a postcard, drop me a line,
    |**G** |
Stating point of view.
G7 | |
Indicate precisely what you mean to say,
N.C. |**C** |
Yours sincerely, wasting away.
     | |
Give me your answer, fill in a form,
C7 |**F** |
Mine for ever - more.
    Fm |**C**   **A** |
Will you still need me, will you still feed me
D7   **G7** |**C**   **G**   **C** ‖
When I'm sixty - four?

Outro

C | |**F** **G** |**C** **G** **C**‖